This planner belongs to

_____

_____

Date

Unless otherwise indicated, all Scripture quotations are taken from the Holy Bible, New International Version®, NIV®. Copyright © 1973, 1978, 1984, 2011 by Biblica, Inc.® Used by permission. All rights reserved worldwide.

Cover design by Emily Weigel Design

Interior design by Chad Dougherty

Cover photo © Rorygez Fresh, Kate Aedon, lily2014, Madiwaso / Shutterstock

Interior illustrations by Lemonade Pixel / Creative Market

Published in association with Books & Such Literary Management, 5926 Sunhawk Drive, Santa Rosa, CA 95409, www.booksandsuch.com.

Portions of the content were previously published in *Get Yourself Organized for Christmas*.

The Christmas Project Planner
Copyright © 2015, 2019 by Kathi Lipp
Published by Harvest House Publishers
Eugene, Oregon 97408
www.harvesthousepublishers.com

ISBN 978-0-7369-7821-7 (pbk.)

Printed in China

HARVEST HOUSE PUBLISHERS
EUGENE, OREGON

19 20 21 22 23 24 25 26 27 / RDS-CD / 10 9 8 7 6 5 4 3 2 1

YOUR

21 PROJECTS

FOR A

CLUTTER-FREE

Christmas

Contents

ELF OR GRINCH:
YOU GET TO CHOOSE

I think there are two kinds of Christmas extremists.

First, there's your friend who has a selection of ugly Christmas sweaters to choose from for every party. She's the one, first in line, waiting outside of Target on December 26 to stock up on all things Christmas themed. She has formal, semiformal, and casual Christmas dishes. All of her neighbors have come together and submitted footage of the outside of her house for "The Best Christmas Display Ever" on TLC. I am not that woman.

Second, there's your other friend who wants to huddle in the corner where the Christmas tree should have been, rocking back and forth and waiting for the sweet release of January 1 to finally come. I have been that woman.

I pray you fall somewhere in between.

Whether you are filled with magical Christmas wonder or extreme Christmas dread, one thing is for certain: Ready or not, Christmas is going to happen. And if you're reading this book, my guess is that the thought that Christmas is going to happen fills you with a mixture of delight and dread.

I doubt Christmas is the problem. It's the expectations around Christmas that are killing you slowly.

The shopping, hosting, wrapping, shipping, cooking, designing, decorating, mailing, entertaining, and baking may all be things you enjoy. But when there's a time limit, a money limit, and, let's be honest, an energy limit, the things you love can start to turn into things you dread.

That's why I'm here to help.

You see, I've been there. I was the woman waiting in line at Target, spending twice my annual income to buy stocking stuffers (that my kids were going to spend exactly 33 seconds unpacking).

I was the woman who stayed up every night until midnight for a week to bake Magical Christmas Cookie Bars for a cookie exchange I never wanted to be a part of. (One woman actually showed up with Hydrox cookies she wanted to exchange for my magical cookies. I may have lost my Christmas joy ever so momentarily…)

***

Whether you are filled with magical wonder or dread, one thing is for certain: Ready or not, Christmas is going to happen.

I was the woman who had a full-on mental break because I ran out of clear tape on Christmas Eve.

And I didn't want to be that woman anymore. In fact, I really didn't like her much.

So I went through a few years of trying to figure out exactly what I wanted my Christmas (and my family's Christmas) to look like.

I wanted to keep the annual viewing of the neighborhood lights (after driving through Starbucks for a Christmas latte) but ditch the crumbly cookie exchange.

I wanted to read the Christmas story but not feel obligated to tell our story in a Christmas letter every single year.

I wanted to have some time just with my husband to celebrate the holiday instead of making him wait until December 31 to reconnect with his wife.

And I want you to have the kind of Christmas you love.

I want you to have the kind of Christmas where you celebrate the things that are truly important to you: faith, family, friends. (And, for me, throw in a little fun and food, and you've got yourself a truly magical holiday.)

I want you to put aside the expectations of what you "should do" and truly dig into what you want to do this Christmas season.

And let's be clear: This isn't about one day. I don't want you to just get to *the* day and then collapse in an utter heap of exhaustion. I want you to have joy, peace, and a plan for the *whole* holiday season.

I think having an organized Christmas is important. But what I really want for you is to have a Christmas that is clutter-free. Free of emotional, physical, and relational clutter.

So as we together work our way through the 21 projects in this book, I will be giving you tips to keep down the clutter in your Christmas.

> ### ✳✳✳
> I want you to have the kind of Christmas where you celebrate the things that are truly important to you: faith, family, friends.

When I asked my friends what a clutter-free Christmas would look like, here is one of my favorite responses. Fellow author Jill Davis was forced to look at every area of her holiday celebration after her life took a decidedly different direction:

When I got divorced eight years ago and had to make huge changes in life with my four children, I asked them what was most important to them. We chose two traditions—the Advent calendar and sugar cookies, plus their favorite gifts of pajamas and a book on Christmas Eve. So much easier than all the shopping, baking, cleaning, and decorating I used to do. Instead of having a beautifully decorated home, fabulous things to eat, lots of Christmas presents, and a frantic mom, they now have an easygoing, low-key, lightly decorated Christmas with a very present mom. Life is better. Christmas is easier. We are all happier.

A clutter-free Christmas says we are doing only those things that are truly important. We are not getting weighed down by unnecessary expenditures, obligations, or craziness.

A BRIEF WORD ABOUT THE PROJECTS

You may be picking this book up on October 5. Good for you. You have a head start on all the projects.

Or maybe your best friend just pressed this book into your hand on December 9. Okay. Take a deep breath. You can double up on some of the projects and then store this book with your fall decorations so you're ahead of the game for next year.

Whenever you begin (and if you have a choice, I would aim to start around the beginning or middle of November), I promise you'll make it through.

If you're getting a late start, it's even more important to do only the things that truly need to be done. In other words, skip the Christmas letter but save the Christmas fudge. (It's important to have our priorities straight.) There are no gold stars for people who complete all 21 projects. The best reward? Creating the Christmas you and your family actually want.

And no matter when you start, let me be 100 percent absolutely crystal clear: You have my full permission (and blessing) to skip some of the projects.

Please hear me on this.

I do not do all the projects every year—and I literally wrote the book.

One of the most freeing things you can do is go through this planner and figure out all the projects you are *not* going to do.

You'll even find a few catch-up days to do the things that need to get done.

Don't worry. You've got this.

THREE STEPS TO KICK OFF
YOUR CHRISTMAS RIGHT

*E*xpectations.

 If there is anything that can make your Christmas a holiday to dread, it is expectations. Others' expectations.

Expectations of how things should be.

Your expectations of yourself.

A year is a long time between celebrations. In that time, you may have forgotten certain small details.

Details like how no one in the family ate any of your cranberry cheese mold (the one that took up an entire shelf in your fridge for nine hours). Or how everyone loved it when you showed the JibJab video of your family with "Rockin' Around the Christmas Tree." And they can't wait to see what video you are showing this year.

I know that when it comes to expectations, the one who is usually putting the most pressure on me is myself. Because everything that everyone has ever enjoyed at our holiday celebration—I want to make THAT happen again. (People pleaser much?)

So, I say, let's all deal with those expectations right up front.

1 First, find out what's actually important to the family or close friends you celebrate Christmas with.

One year, after being exhausted by all the demands for different types of food each of my kids had told me we *had* to have, I finally asked them, "Tell me what's truly important to you."

Their answer? Pumpkin cheesecake.

That's what was important to everyone. The no-bake cheesecake Roger makes every year. That was the deepest desire of my kids' hearts.

So this time, I didn't make a 12-helping recipe of every food that every mom and grandma in our family has made for the last 30 years. We made the meal, had some family favorites, and made the cheesecake.

It was simple, and everyone was happy. (For the most part. Hey, it's not a magical cheesecake.)

In other words, ask people in advance what they want, and when reasonable (and it's something you would enjoy doing or can assign to someone else), you do it. But you don't add one single thing to you list because you *should* do it.

Second, figure out what's actually important to you.

When we're in charge of making Christmas miracles, we are so busy creating the Christmas everyone else wants that we forget to step back and look at what's actually important and meaningful to us.

I want you to imagine for a moment not the perfect Christmas, but what you want Christmas to feel like. Peaceful? Joyous? Comfortable? Figure out what's important to you, and then plan toward that.

If you want a peaceful Christmas, but you're still making 16 different kinds of cookies (and you lost your love of baking right after the snickerdoodles and the fudgy fantastic flourless cookies), then your plan is at odds with what's important to you.

Third, make a list of how others can help.

Last year, I made an amazing discovery about my husband. He is not in the least offended when I tell him what to do. In fact, he appreciates it.

This revelation occurred when we were both waiting for our coffee to brew. As I was waiting, I was unloading the dishwasher, wiping down the counters, and refilling the water bowl for the dog.

> ✳ ✳ ✳
>
> When we're in charge of making Christmas miracles, we are so busy creating the Christmas everyone else wants that we forget to step back and look at what's important and meaningful to us.

And Roger?

He was standing there.

At first I was a little irritated. (Okay, downright "Are. You. Kidding. Me?" might be a better description…) How could he just stand there while I was working? Shouldn't he want to help?

So I asked him, "Hey, could you put away the silverware?"

And he said, "Sure!"

We discussed it later, and I found out he honestly didn't notice that anything needed to be done. "I'm always willing to do this stuff," he said, "but sometimes I just don't think of it."

So now, after dinner, we have a new ritual. Roger does dishes, my least-favorite part of kitchen cleanup. With dishes, it's straightforward, and there aren't a lot of decisions to be made. And while he's doing dishes, I'm putting food away, taking the dirty towels to the laundry, wiping down counters, and so on.

The difference? I see what needs to be done. In this relationship, I am the seer.

And that's a lot like Christmas. You probably have a natural instinct about what needs to be done for Christmas. Others in your family? Not so much. You are the seer.

My husband is always happy to help. But when it comes to Christmas, he needs a little direction.

Every year we have people over for our celebration, and the most common question is, "How can I help?" (I only invite really nice people over.) In the heat of the moment (and in the heat of the kitchen), I'm almost always at a loss for how to direct people on how to assist.

So for the past few years, I've done something different. As I made my checklists of Christmas prep (for the season) and meal and party prep (for the day), I highlighted anything that someone else could do.

So when guests asked in advance, "What can I bring?" or "Is there any way I can help?" I was able to look at my list and say, "Yep. Could you pick up ice on your way here?" Or, "We're short on appetizers. I would love for you to bring your famous cheddar cheese puffs!"

And on the day of the event, when people wandered into the kitchen and asked, "How can I help?" I was able to look at my list and say, "You can chop the celery for the stuffing," or "I would love for you to put out the cheese-and-cracker plate. Here's everything you'll need."

(As the years have advanced and I've become even smarter, like the Christmas wonder that I am, I now have all the cheese in one plastic bag and all the cracker boxes on the plate that I want them to be put on. This is ninja-level Christmas prep—something to aspire to…)

By spending 15 extra minutes thinking through what others can do, you're going to save yourself not only time but also wear and tear. (And it will keep you from passing out on the couch before dessert…)

Here's your short list:

1. Find out what's actually important to people you love.

2. Take a moment to think about what's important to you.

3. Be prepared to ask for (and receive) help.

I promise. You've just made your Christmas 32 percent happier.

· PROJECT 1 ·

WHY PLANNING IS AWESOME

It is my deepest hope that no one feels like a failure around Christmastime. I've felt that way myself too many times to count, and for you and for me that stops now.

I think of all those times I started dreaming about Christmas in late October or early November and thought everything was possible. I was going to throw the parties, make the meals, send the cards, arrange the cookie exchanges, and generally just crush Christmas.

But my vague notions of what Christmas should look like rarely translated into the Festival of Awesomeness I'd imagined. Because, sadly, the world doesn't take a break for Christmas. Time to prep and plan? Nobody is getting any time off to plan the perfect Christmas.

So what's a mere mortal to do? Just try your best to have a good Christmas and figure it out as you go?

That usually doesn't work. Instead of engaging in crisis control the entire Christmas season, you can actually go in with a plan—not so much about what you want to do but what you don't need to worry about.

Start planning now, and you will experience a more sacred and sane holiday this year. Promise!

> ***
> My vague notions of what Christmas should look like rarely translated into the Festival of Awesomeness I'd imagined.

Create Your Christmas Plan

Here's what you will need:

- two or three index cards
- a marker
- My Holiday Mission Statement form (see page 19)

> ***
> Being intentional about how we spend our time and our physical and emotional energy is the key to a more sane and sacred celebration.

I know, I know. You want to dive in and start checking things off your list because it's going to be a busy few weeks. I get it. But first I want you to spend ten minutes determining this: *What do you want your Christmas to look like this year?*

If we can go into the holidays being intentional about everything—how we spend our time and our physical and emotional energy—it truly will be the key to a more sane and sacred celebration.

On the Holiday Mission Statement, I want you to spend some time thinking about what you want your season of celebration to look like. Here are some words that might spark some thoughts:

time	growth	reflect	restore
energy	tradition	honor	food
priorities	creating	provide	peace
spiritual	patience	creativity	joy
friends	gift giving	love	self-control
family	commitment	cherish	serve
travel	community	activities	together
focus	charity	include	connect
celebrate	church	God	care

Brainstorm about what is important to you. Some years, I'm looking for joy. I want to experience the deep, abiding joy that only comes from God and being with His people.

Several years ago, it was different: I was all about peace. Between chaos in my ministry, chaos in our home lives, chaos in my husband's job, and a triple shot of chaos with my mom's health, I needed the peace that passes understanding. Here is what my mission statement looked like for that year:

I will share God's peace with my family, my friends, and people I meet, and I will be done with my prep by December 20 so that I can experience peace during our celebration. I will read the Christmas story each morning in December.

And yes, God delivered that—even while at the mall. In December.

How did He deliver that?

After some prayer, I felt God had given us permission to take several things off our list. I bought favorite cookies instead of making them. No cards went out that year (but I sure enjoyed the ones I received). We didn't go to a lot of events, and we didn't have people over for dinner, but we went out with some dear friends who could let us just be us amid all the chaos.

Also, all the adults agreed that year to not exchange gifts. I did get something for my parents, but my brother and sister-in-law and Roger and I agreed that this was a year to reduce the time, energy, and money it took to buy for one another.

The next year, here is what I wanted my Christmas to look like:

During this Christmas season, I want to throw off old traditions that are just habits and do those things that:

- *bring me closer to God*
- *bring us together as a family*
- *equip us to serve*

With a healthy mom (thank God!) and a restoring of a little bit of normalcy to our lives, we doubled down on creating a Christmas we would all want. Roger was able to serve at church, and I was able to concentrate on having family and friends to our home to connect with and love on.

Once you know what is important to you, you can figure out how you're going to get there.

Once you figure out your why, then you can start figuring out your how. And here's where those index cards and marker come in handy. This is what I wrote:

> *I will ask in advance for help from my family (spouse, parents, sibling, kids). In order to remind myself (and those I love) about this Christmas plan, I'm putting it on an index card in three places:*
>
> - *on the fridge*
> - *on my computer*
> - *on the visor of my car*

(And yes, these are the three places where I need a little more Jesus during the holidays.)

I've been doing a Holiday Mission Statement since 2011, and it has made a huge change in how I approach the holidays.

Three years ago, my Holiday Mission Statement was simple. I wanted to experience joy amid sorrow. My dad passed away September 5. We were all still processing the loss and what that looked like to our family.

> ✳✳✳
> Doing a Holiday Mission Statement has made a huge change in how I approach the holidays.

But there were also some opportunities for joy—sharing memories, eating some of his favorite foods, and loving on each other. We kept the celebration easy (celebrating on December 26, only three gifts for each of our kids, and a Secret Santa gift exchange for our extended family). While it was nothing that HGTV would feature in an *Elegant Extravagance Holiday Special*, it was perfect for our family and the place we were in. We gave ourselves a pass on anything that wasn't necessary, and we just loved on each other, played games, went to church, and remembered what was special in our lives.

It was, I daresay, the perfect Christmas.

NOW IT'S YOUR TURN...

It's time to start brainstorming about what your Holiday Mission Statement should look like. It doesn't need to be perfect; it just needs to focus you. Once you've got it down, write it on the form on page 19 so you can refer to it. (And don't forget to copy it to the places where you will need to be reminded about keeping the holiday spirit—on your fridge, next to your computer, and in your wallet are just a few of the places you may need a little reminder.)

Now that you've decided what you want your Christmas to look like, it's important that you don't let all the holiday madness sneak back in. You get to decide exactly how crazy this season is. If you truly want to have an on-purpose Christmas, it starts with how you spend your time, energy, and money. When you stick to your Christmas mission, you are saying the world doesn't get a say in how you celebrate.

- If you're having a hard time coming up with your mission statement, step back for a day and think on it. This idea is not to add stress to your life—it's to focus you for the season so you can truly bless others and receive the blessings.

- Still stuck? Maybe you're stuck trying to make it the perfect Holiday Mission Statement. If that's the case, aim for 80 percent. Write your mission statement on page 19 in pencil and then give yourself permission to go back and change about 20 percent later on. It's your mission statement. You get to decide how it goes.

Christmas QUICK TIPS

What kind of Christmas do you want—or maybe need—this year? Step back, think about it, and plan for it now.

Holiday Mission Statement

THIS IS WHAT I WANT CHRISTMAS TO LOOK LIKE THIS YEAR:

....

....

....

....

....

....

....

....

....

....

....

....

....

....

HOW TO MAKE A MAGIC CHRISTMAS BOX THAT WILL BE BETTER THAN ANY ELF

When I was in the seventh grade, I saved all my babysitting money to buy, not a pair of Keds or a Madonna tape, but four Trapper Keeper binders. Yes, four. One for school, one to keep track of my babysitting jobs, one for notes and such, and the last one…well, just in case one of the other ones broke or went missing.

Now you may be thinking that I was a bit geeky. Who chooses an office product over new shoes? But in reality, it was pure brilliance.

When you have all your stuff in one place, you can easily keep track of it. And seventh-grade Kathi seemed to innately know what I now know for a fact: The first step to any great project is getting your thoughts together and all in one place.

And today's project does just that—gets your Christmas all in one place so you can be organized and ready for whatever the season throws at you.

Create Your Christmas Prep Space

I want you to create a safe place to keep all your Christmas stuff.

If you're like most people, you have your recipes in various cookbooks, a bunch of envelopes from last year's Christmas cards stuffed into a kitchen drawer, and your Christmas stamps attached to your fridge with a magnet.

It's time to stop the madness.

You've already taken the first completely organized step: You have this book in your hand.

I mean, how great is this book? With its pockets and planning tools and All. The. Things? Don't you already feel a TON more organized?

But if your Christmas is anything like mine, it can't fit into just one book. You're gonna need a space. Not a big space, but just a tiny corner of the world that is basically your Christmas command center.

First, I want you to start pulling all your loose papers, Christmas labels, lists, recipes, and any other holiday-related paraphernalia into one place.

Then decide what your Christmas Prep and Plan Container is going to look like. Mine is a file box with a handle and a couple of file folders I can tote around the house with me, but I can also put it away in my office when I'm finished. It's big enough to hold everything I need: recipes, mailing labels, scissors, lists, coupons, gift cards, and so on.

When you have everything Christmas-related in one place, it's going to make it a lot easier to find your favorite pumpkin custard recipe or the receipt for the Barbie toothbrush your daughter just said "is for babies" and needs to go back to the store.

This is probably your first year creating your Christmas Plan and Prep Container. It's probably a nice, small little file box, shoe box, or whatever, and it's totally manageable. But as the years go on, you are going to be throwing a lot of things into that container. Make sure at the beginning of every holiday season that you clear out everything you won't need: old envelopes, leftover Christmas cards, and Pinterest ideas that looked fun in the moment but you know will never see the light of day (because who is really going to create a Christmas wreath out of old Diet Coke cans?).

While putting together your container, add only those things you will really use. One of the secrets of keeping the system usable is to keep it uncluttered.

- Make sure to spend a few minutes on your container every day throughout the holiday season.

- When Christmas is over, store your portable file box for next year as is. You may end up throwing out some of the stuff, but you'll already have a good start on next year's holidays.

I promise you that this box will save you so much time, stress, and angst during the Christmas season.

STRIKE A POSE

I have mixed feelings about getting Christmas cards and letters.

The ones from good friends with pictures of a cute couple, kids, and dog, and sweet notes about what's been going on the past year? Adore.

The ones with the detailed list of accomplishments and how everyone in the family is a part of Mensa and the middle-school son has just been drafted into the NFL? Pass.

I love some humor, some highlights, and some truth. That's the kind of Christmas card and letter I want to receive.

Now, let's talk about sending cards. Let me be the first to say that I don't think sending a Christmas card is a requirement for being a good mom, wife, daughter, or friend. I have several people in my life I've never received a card from, and I still adore them.

That being said, I do love receiving those cards and pictures. If you are one of my friends who sends them, thank you. Keep those cards coming.

And I don't always send them. No cards went out the year I had a book due, my mom had cancer, and I had whooping cough all in the same two-week span. If you are having that kind of holiday season, you get a Christmas card pass. If you'd like, I can even write you a note. (Like the ones your mom wrote to get you out of gym class when you felt icky enough to want to stay home from school but had to go anyway. Thanks, Mom.)

So if you've decided not to send a photo in your cards (or not even send a card at all) this year, go do something fun, like watch *Elf* or have a cup of cocoa with a friend. For the rest of you, you have a job to do. But it's a fun one: Today, I want you to pick the picture that's going to go on your card.

Pick Your Christmas Card Picture

You actually have a choice of assignments today. You can either:

- Pick your Christmas picture (if you're including one in your cards).
- Set a date to take a family picture.

See? Fun and easy. If you already have the photo on your phone, computer, or in the cloud, you can send it to Costco, Target, or your online personalized card company (we've had great results from Shutterfly.com) to create your cards. But for today, just enjoy looking through all those pics on your computer (or your phone) and remembering how blessed you and yours have been this year.

What kind of photo do you want? Professional, candid snapshot, or something you found from this summer? Anything goes when it comes to today's Christmas cards. You no longer need to bundle up in matching sweaters and borrow someone's golden retriever to be legit.

Our Christmas photos are always less than perfect. One year we had no decent pics of our whole family together, so we just did a collage. A couple of years ago we had an adorable picture of our whole family in the snow—except my daughter Kimber was holding an ice scraper. I thought about Photoshopping it out or not using the picture, but every time I see that picture, I remember that it snowed so much in Lake Tahoe that we barely escaped spending the next week in our rented cabin. And just as we were digging out our cars, my brother gathered us all together to take that picture. I love it for all the memories it has for me and our family.

That is what I call a perfect picture. Ice scraper and all.

> ✳✳✳
>
> For today, just enjoy looking through all those pics on your computer and remembering how blessed you and yours have been this year.

Want some suggestions for getting great family shots? Here are some been-there-done-that ideas:

Relax and have fun with it.

Everyone SMILE!

Remember that location, location, location is important.

Dress the part.

Consider hiring a photographer.

Don't leave family photography to the last minute. Love a pro photo from a friend's Christmas card? Ask her who took it and bookmark the photographer's site. Adore a friend's Facebook profile picture? Fan the photographer on Facebook and see whose images really connect with you over the course of the year. Most photographers' calendars fill up early in this busy portrait season, so start looking for fall specials, or reserve your date when summer is starting to wrap up, long before the cool weather hits. If you're going with a professional photographer, be sure to choose one based on the way their images make you feel.

We are better throughout the year

for having, in spirit,

become a child again at Christmastime.

—Laura Ingalls Wilder

SUPPORT YOUR LOCAL POST OFFICE!

Remember, you are no less of a Christmas elf if you end up not sending Christmas cards. In fact, try this little experiment:

Sit back, close your eyes, and tell yourself, "I'm not sending Christmas cards this year."

How did that make you feel?

Sad?

Relieved?

Ashamed?

Free to live the life that is intended for you?

If you are leaning toward relieved and free, would you consider, seriously, not sending them out? Maybe next year you'll actually look forward to it.

Prep Your Christmas Cards

However, if you are going to send them out, there are a few steps you need to take:

- Pick your Christmas cards.
- Gather up mailing addresses.
- Organize addresses.
- Print addresses.
- Order stamps.
- Get your return address stamp or stickers, or have your return address printed on the envelopes.

Look at all those steps. No wonder many of us quit in the middle.

So today, all I want you to do is create a folder on your computer, select your Christmas cards, gather the addresses you plan on sending cards to, and order or pick up your stamps.

The first thing is create a folder on your computer called "Christmas." This is where everything for your Christmas celebration will go that you need to store on your computer. Next Christmas, you will find this book, open this computer folder, and you'll have everything you need for your Christmas.

Addresses

For addresses, get any envelopes and lists from last year, your address book, and your online address book. Create an Excel spreadsheet with all the info you will need. (You'll be super grateful next year when you don't have to handwrite all those addresses again.)

Create your list.

This may take a couple of sessions, but have no fear, I've put a couple of work sessions into these projects! Once you get your list together, you'll be able to either hand address your envelopes or create a Mail Merge from your Excel list. You can find a great tutorial on "How to Create a Mail Merge" at www.gcflearnfree.org/word2013/31/print. It will take a time or two to learn, but it's a great skill to have. And if you want to make labels and Mail Merge scares you, ask a friend for help—and then bake some cookies for her.

***

Next Christmas, you will find this book, open this computer folder, and you'll have everything you need for your Christmas.

Pick a Card, Any Card

As far as cards go, all you have to do is make your decision between custom cards or store bought. Yes, custom are cute. Store bought are great for those who might be late getting started.

Order Stamps

Don't wait to get your stamps until the week before and then have to wait in line at the post office. You can have stamps delivered to your mailbox by going through USPS.com. Order the theme you want, pay online, and have them waiting for you when your cards are ready to go!

Saving Money, Santa Style

One year, I took all my leftover Christmas cards and sent those out instead of buying new ones. I put in a simple letter with an update on our family and sent them on their way. Did anyone notice that they got the same card from us two years in a row? Maybe, though probably not. But who cares? I used up a bunch of cards and saved some cash. Plus, I still had leftovers after that, which I used as gift tags.

Cull Your Christmas Card List

Just because you sent a card to someone you cared about 12 years ago doesn't mean you have to send them a card every year. This should not be a life sentence. One of my friends does a big blowout card to everyone on her list every five years and sends cards just to close friends and family the other years.

If you are one of those women who said she wanted a simpler Christmas, may I politely suggest an adorable, standard-sized, store-bought card? (And if you're making your cards from scratch, I can't even talk with you.)

- Make sure to hang on to cards that are returned because of a wrong address and update your address file on your computer. So much better than sending cards to the wrong address five years in a row.

- Put your stamps in the front pocket of this book. (I can't even tell you how many times I have put my stamps someplace safe only to find them January 5.)

You merry folk, be of good cheer,

For Christmas comes but once a year.

From open door you'll take no harm

By winter if your hearts are warm.

—Geoffrey Smith

EVEN SANTA HAS A STRATEGY

Okay, it's time to kick the Christmas plans into high gear. Spend 15 minutes scheduling all your commitments for the next few weeks on the calendar.

It's so easy to have great ideas ("Let's go look at Christmas lights!" or "Let's curl up and watch *Elf* one night this week!") and let them all slip through your fingers because of the Christmas Crazies. So, along with all the chores of the season, let's schedule in some fun!

> ✳✳✳
> It's so easy to have great ideas and let them all slip through your fingers because of the Christmas Crazies.

Schedule Your Time for the Holidays

Here's what you will need:

- the November and December calendar pages in this planner (see pages 34 through 37)
- school calendars
- church calendars
- work calendars
- personal calendars

I love that you can keep everything for the holidays right here in this planner—including your November and December calendars. Here are some things you may want to consider with your schedule:

- kids' school calendar
- kids' other activities (sports, dance, theater)
- work events
- church events
- parties and other fun

Once you've filled in all the already-scheduled activities, set aside some pockets of time to work on prepping for Christmas. Here are some things you may want to schedule some time for:

- getting a tree
- cookie baking
- decorating
- project nights (for wrapping, card addressing, ordering gifts online)
- a night to look at Christmas lights
- a night to watch *It's a Wonderful Life*

I'm not saying you should do all of those things (in fact, I don't think you should), but if you want to do any of these or any other family or friend activities, put them on your calendar in advance so you can plan around them. (Because any free time around the holidays will be sucked up like the last marshmallow dream bar at the office Christmas party.)

Try taking one activity off your calendar that you "always" do but which may have lost some of its meaning. I used to do an Advent calendar every year. It was big and cute and had 24 pockets at the bottom, each holding a wrapped ornament for my kids to take turns placing on a big felt tree.

***
Try taking one activity off your calendar that you "always" do but which may have lost some of its meaning.

One year I brought it out, hung it up, and announced to my 11-year-old, Justen, that it was his turn to unwrap the Advent surprise. "Is there money in there?" he asked.

"Um, no…"

"Okay. Then just let Kimmy do it."

I was crushed.

Truth was, Justen didn't care about the Advent calendar, and after a couple of years, neither did Kimber. Yes, we still celebrated Advent, but they were past the age of wanting to unwrap knickknacks every morning for a month.

I put away the Advent tree, a little sad but also realizing that it still had a future. Seven years later, my brother had a daughter, Elsa, who now does the Advent tree. Someday, Elsa will outgrow it, probably about the time my kids start having kids, and the tradition can continue.

More to Christmas

There's more, much more, to Christmas
Than candlelight and cheer;
It's the spirit of sweet friendship,
That brightens all the year.
It's thoughtfulness and kindness,
It's hope reborn again,
For peace, for understanding
And for goodwill to men!

Author Unknown

- Limit the number of kid activities each of your children are participating in. Lots of excitement mixed with equal parts sugar can wreak havoc with your schedule.

- Make sure you have a couple at-home nights every week to just be with your people. You will need some downtime to really enjoy the rest of the week without feeling frantic.

- When you're snuggled up on the couch with your family, eating fresh-baked cookies while watching *It's a Wonderful Life*, you'll thank me.

NOVEMBER

SUNDAY	MONDAY	TUESDAY	WEDNESDAY

THURSDAY	FRIDAY	SATURDAY	NOTES

☐

☐

☐

....

....

....

....

☐

☐

☐

....

....

....

....

☐

☐

☐

....

....

....

....

☐

☐

☐

....

....

....

....

☐

☐

☐

....

....

....

....

☐

☐

☐

DECEMBER

SUNDAY	MONDAY	TUESDAY	WEDNESDAY
☐	☐	☐	☐
☐	☐	☐	☐
☐	☐	☐	☐
☐	☐	☐	☐
☐	☐	☐	☐
☐	☐	☐	☐

THURSDAY	FRIDAY	SATURDAY	NOTES
☐	☐	☐	....
☐	☐	☐	....
☐	☐	☐	....
☐	☐	☐	....
☐	☐	☐	....
☐	☐	☐	

· PROJECT 6 ·

WHO'S BEEN NAUGHTY OR NICE?

My daughter, Kimber, has gift-giving anxiety.

Actually, for her it's more like gift-receiving anxiety.

Kimber is a sensitive girl and hates the thought of hurting anyone's feelings. She also is a terrible liar, which, when she was a teenager, was a blessing for this mom. As a gift receiver? It's a huge handicap.

As we'd all gather around the tree to open gifts, grandparents would wait anxiously to see the look of delight on Kimber's face as she opened the scarf they'd bought her or the notebook she'd described wanting.

But Kimber is not one for whom any old scarf will do. It needs to be the *exact* scarf she saw at H&M or the notebook with the college-ruled paper and the black cover. So when her honest reaction was less than utter joy, Kimber felt put on the spot and judged.

We've eliminated all that now. She gives me a list of links to the things she wants. (To be totally honest, she also gives me her Sephora Beauty Insiders Loyalty Program number so that she can earn free gifts from my purchase. Her theory is, why would you let any of that go to waste?) You would think this would eliminate the Christmas magic. It does not. For me to be able to give a gift that my daughter truly wants is a wonderful thing for her—and for me. I am not about surprise, but I am all about delight.

> *******
>
> For me to be able to give a gift that my daughter truly wants is a wonderful thing for her— and for me.

Get Your Gift List Together

For this project, write out all your gift ideas and what gifts you've already bought.

You'll find the Gift Idea Command Center on pages 42 and 43.

Wouldn't it be great if the gift-giving part of Christmas was the least stressful? Here are a few ideas to help you take the stress off:

Limit the List

For several years, we limited the number of gifts we bought for each kid: one spiritual gift, one clothing gift, and one fun gift. You may think that sounds very *Little House on the Prairie*-ish, but with all the grandparents, aunts and uncles, and friends, the kids weren't hurting for gifts. Trust me. We plan to limit gifts again this year now that all the kids are adults and bringing other people into the family (through marriage).

Extended Family Swap

We're doing this with my extended family this year. We used Elfster.com, and my step-daughter, Amanda, registered all of us through Facebook. You can be registered through an e-mail address as well. The website automatically assigns you a person, and then that person can make gift suggestions and put links to the items on Amazon or other online retailers. This is especially helpful if the person assigned to you is someone you don't spend every day with or, if they're like Kimber, only the Urban Decay Born to Run Eyeshadow Palette will do. Having the link to a website where I can order the correct brand and item? Priceless.

> ***
> If a family gift swap is something you want to try, talk about it with your family now, not the week of Christmas.

Every time I start to panic about not having a gift for my brother, I stop, take a deep breath, and remember—"He's not on my list this year." Huzzah! If this is something you want to try, talk about it with your family now, not the week of Christmas.

Ask

Ask people what they would like. I know it's fun to surprise people with something perfect, but really, why stress yourself out?

Keep Your Ears Open

Have a Post-it page for each of the main people you buy for, and start taking notes. Maybe your son mentioned a book he's interested in or your husband received a renewal notice for his favorite magazine. Make a quick note to get it, or jot it down for next year.

Also, be sure to check out friends' and family's Amazon Wish List. A couple of times I've been able to surprise someone with something they put on their list and then totally forgot about. It makes you seem like a Christmas magician with special powers.

Stalk Them on Social Media

Some of my best gift ideas this past year came from things my family posted on social media. My daughter talked about a cookie she was obsessed with, and my son put a link to some *Star Wars* posters he was in love with. With both of them being broke, I knew neither of them would be purchasing those items for themselves, so they made great Christmas gifts.

> ✳✳✳
>
> Some of my best gift ideas came from things my family posted on social media.

Give to Charity

One thing we love to do is give a charitable gift in the name of those friends and relatives who always say, "Don't buy me anything. I already have too much stuff!" Here are some ways to honor someone through a charitable gift:

- If they are an animal lover, give to a local animal shelter.

- If they love kids, donate to a children's charity, such as Compassion International.

- A local food bank is always a great option for a contribution. Think about making the donation in the town where they grew up.

Try to limit your list. I'm not saying kick people off completely, but think outside the wrapped Christmas box for some other ideas:

- If you know that someone in your family or group is struggling financially, could you suggest that you all take a year's reprieve from gift giving? There's nothing worse (I know from personal experience) than being the broke one in the family and having to come up with Christmas miracles for everyone.

- When my kids were younger, they had more time than money and would give their grandparents the gift of several hours of chores around the house. Instead of giving my parents another knickknack they didn't need, my daughter gave them six hours of garage and house cleaning. Not only did my mom love the help, but she also loved the time she got to spend with her granddaughter.

- For large groups that might be tempted to exchange gifts, what if you went out for lunch instead? No one feels left out, and you all get to enjoy each other's company. Double win.

Gift Idea Command Center

GIFT RECIPIENT	GIFT IDEA
....	....
....	....
....	....
....	....
....	....
....	....
....	....
....	....
....	....
....	....
....	....
....	....
....	....
....	....

Gift Idea Command Center

GIFT RECIPIENT	GIFT IDEA
....	....
....	....
....	....
....	....
....	....
....	....
....	....
....	....
....	....
....	....
....	....
....	....
....	....

· PROJECT 7 ·

CAN I ASK SANTA TO PAY OFF MY VISA CARD?

I want you to avoid the Christmas hangover.

No. I'm not talking about monitoring your intake of eggnog (which, by the way, is not a bad idea if that's your thing). I want you to avoid the financial hangover so many of us have in January.

> ***
>
> At no other time of year does the mentality of "buy now, pay later" dominate more than during the month of December.

At no other time of year does the mentality of "eat now, diet later" or "buy now, pay later" dominate more than during the month of December. It's as if we're all a bunch of first graders whose teacher left the classroom, and we're gonna have as much fun as humanly possible until teacher gets back, and then may God have mercy on our souls.

We need to budget our time and money in a way that says, "Here's how I'm being intentional about what I spend and what I spend it on." If we're making a magical Christmas with late nights and overdrawn accounts, the magic only lasts so long.

Creating a Christmas Budget

Here's what you will need:

The Budgeting Sheets (see pages 48 and 49)

Yes, it's a big holiday, and for most of us, it makes up a huge part of our fall and winter expenses. So I want you to spend a little time budgeting what you are going to spend. Here are some areas that you may want to consider:

food	clothes	holiday tips (for hairdresser, housecleaner, postal worker)
gifts	cards	
donations	shipping	
decorations	travel	

Have a discussion with your husband or whomever you share the money with. I'm not telling you what to budget; I just don't want you to be surprised at the end of the month.

Trying to get your Dave Ramsey on this holiday season? Here are some things to think about:

- Eliminate some categories altogether. How about this year instead of shipping gifts, you send gift cards to your out-of-town relatives? Or maybe skip the Christmas cards this year and save some serious cash when it comes to cards, the photo, labels, and stamps.

- Do you really need new clothes for the holidays? Don't you have a great outfit from two winters ago buried in the back of your closet? How about some friends you might be able to trade hand-me-downs with for your kids' clothes? Get creative and see if that can be a zero-budget item for you.

- If you host the family dinner every year, realize that every dish you ask someone else to bring could be saving you between $10 and $20. Plus, this also makes people feel more a part of the celebration instead of invited guests.

- Are there some people who would be relieved not to exchange gifts this year? Have the discussion as early as possible to see if, instead of presents, you could plan a dinner together at someone's house in January to keep costs down but also to stay connected to people you love.

I asked some of my readers for their best budgeting tips. Here is the genius they shared. May it spark some creative ways for you to do what is important to you and yours without completely blowing your budget.

"I look for sales on the items I want to buy, but even more than that, I like to set aside $50 to $100 a month from the beginning of the year so that I have a big chunk of money to spend just on Christmas. Some banks even have Christmas savings accounts." —*Rachelle*

"Pay cash whenever possible. It is much easier to lose track of your spending and go over budget when using a debit or credit card. By using cash, it's also easier to keep your gift to your spouse a secret if you have a joint account." —*Melody*

"My best advice this time of year is *be patient*. All of those sale signs are enticing, but stores generally offer only a few great deals in an attempt to get you in the door. Don't be tricked into shopping around if you've come just for a deal. Otherwise, you're sure to pay a higher price than you should have on those extras in your cart. Shopping only for the deals takes some time and planning, so start early. Watch for those 'get you in the door' deals, cash in on those, and leave." —*Natasha*

"My siblings and I make donations to World Vision and other worthy organizations instead of sending gifts to one another. We feel good about where the money goes, and we enjoy saving ourselves from the shopping, wrapping, and mailing at Christmas. We do set a certain amount we will spend for each of our children and their spouses. Of course, things will change when they add grandchildren to the equation." —*Sharon*

"We are making gourmet cupcakes for my 13-year-old daughter's teachers and friends. We are putting them in cute boxes I bought for a dollar each. It gives us time together and yummy treats for her friends. It also cuts costs." —*Christie*

"A few years ago we discovered the Advent Conspiracy (www.adventconspiracy.org). They challenge gift givers to focus on what Christ gave us for Christmas: Himself! Instead of buying all kinds of stuff, we now focus on giving our children experiences for us to do together. The other part of the challenge is to take some of the money we would have spent on gifts and give to causes that make a difference in people's lives. Over the last three years, we have given to clean water projects in Guatemala, an orphanage that rescues girls from prostitution in India, and an orphanage in Brazil. Suddenly, that gadget I thought I had to have pales in comparison to these children's basic needs." —*Robin*

Budgeting Sheets

CATEGORIES	BUDGET	ACTUAL

Budgeting Sheets

CATEGORIES	BUDGET	ACTUAL

· PROJECT 8 ·

I PROMISE, YOU'RE NOT BEHIND!

Today is a catch-up day. Use it to catch up on anything you feel you're running behind on. And for extra credit, I have a bonus project that will help you and those you love get into the holiday spirit.

Roger and I have a tradition.

Every year, we each pick a few special items for each other (lotions, superfancy chocolates, a silky robe, silly boxers), wrap them in red paper, and put them under the tree. Nobody else is allowed to be around when the red gifts are unwrapped, and I can say with confidence that our red gifts are hands down our favorite gifts every year. Hands down.

I love this tradition, and I love finding something that will make Roger smile and know he is loved. But as we had our special gift exchange last year, I got to thinking: *Why do I save all my red gifts for Christmas morning when the truth is, I need to pour into my man often? Like every day?*

>
>
> I love finding something that will make Roger smile and know he is loved.

So this year, I'm starting a new tradition. I will, of course, be wrapping a couple of red gifts and putting them under the tree, but I'm also going to do something a little extra once a week in December for Roger to help him know he is loved this Christmas. Nothing big. Just a little something to show him that even though I am crazy busy and the to-do list is a mile long, I still love him first and most.

For today's bonus project, I'm asking you to do the same.

Help Someone Special Get into the Holiday Spirit

Today, I want you to think of one thing you can do for that someone special in your life (a friend, a spouse, a coworker). Maybe it's someone who has had a really tough year. Or maybe it's someone you just know you need to focus on. Try to think of some small (or big!) way you can bless them and show them they are your priority even though the season is getting hectic.

Here are some ideas to get you started as you plan:

- Head to the bakery and buy a Christmas cookie or brownie. Slip it to your special someone and let them know they don't have to share.

- Send them a text to let them know you are thinking of them.

- Take care of a chore they normally do.

- Make hot cocoa and share it by the fire while you talk.

- Rent a Christmas movie and watch it together.

- Whip up their favorite dinner or pick up a favorite food for takeout.

- Offer to shop for their boss or great-aunt. Do it happily without complaining.

DO I LOVE YOU ENOUGH TO ACTUALLY GO TO THE POST OFFICE?

My life was so simple.

Then I married Roger.

You see, my whole family lives within a two-hour drive of my home. We get together for holidays and exchange gifts like the Norman Rockwell painting says we're supposed to do. Then I had to marry a Southern boy.

When Roger was looking for his first grown-up job as a senior at Purdue University, he told God his requirements: "I will go anywhere except California."

Yeah, that's a good idea. Tell God what you *won't* do.

So, many years ago, Roger got a job in Cupertino with HP, and he has been a California boy ever since. The only problem is that his whole family lives in Georgia, and they all celebrate Christmas. And somehow, when we were first married, I forgot that their gifts required an extra step or two.

Today, your project is to get your plan together for any out-of-town gifts. You have three approaches you can take:

1. Order all your gifts online and have them shipped from the company.

2. Buy gifts and ship them from home.

3. Make sure you've married a local boy or stop talking to out-of-state relatives and friends.

Gifts for Out-of-Town Friends and Family

I'm not expecting you to buy and ship all your out-of-town gifts today, but I do want you to think specifically about what you are going to get for whom and by what day you need to have it in the mail.

Think e-gifts for any of your out-of-town relatives and friends. (Think Amazon gift cards, Audible subscriptions, restaurant gift cards, movie tickets, or a subscription to Netflix.) They are easy to send and won't clutter up someone's home. And you don't have to worry about wrapping.

Is there a gift that's easy to mail that everyone would like? Roger's mom sends us and others a selection of nuts from Georgia every year, which we love and look forward to. Keep it simple.

> ***
> Think about what you are going to get for whom and by what day you need to have it in the mail.

My definition of mailable gifts is anything that can be mailed in a bubble envelope or one of the post office's Priority Mail envelopes and get there in the same condition it was mailed in. Here are some ideas of things that are easy to mail.

- *Rubber stamp kit.* For kids, all it takes is a rubber stamp or two, an ink pad, and some paper.

- *T-shirt.* My friend Erin told her kids I was having a bad day (my husband's stepmom had just passed away suddenly) and asked them what they could send me to cheer me up. Joey, her oldest, said, "A UT shirt, of course." Joey naturally assumed that someone he loves would be rooting for the University of Texas. Even though, at the time, I wasn't entirely sure what city UT was in. Oh—and I don't like football. But because it's from Joey, it's my favorite T-shirt ever, and I've worn it for years. And Erin, who has an extreme case of *lukalpostophobia* (an extreme fear of post offices) didn't even have to enter the post office. She just put it in a priority envelope and had it picked up at her house. Genius.

- *Table runner.* I usually shy away from buying things to decorate someone else's house, but a table runner is a small commitment (not something that has to be out every day), and it's easy to mail. I love Pier 1, TJ Maxx, or Cost Plus to find funky ones. A good holiday one is great because it's brought out for only a few days a year.

- *Sharpie markers and fun office supplies.* I am an office supply junkie. I think it calls me back to my youth and those first days of September when I spent hours organizing and reorganizing my school supplies because I was convinced that if I had a perfectly organized binder, it would lead to the Best. Year. Ever.

- *Seeds or bulbs.* How could you better send hope for spring than seeds or bulbs in the mail? It makes my wannabe green thumb itch just thinking about it.

- *Goat from World Vision.* One Christmas my kids got me a sponsorship for a goat for a family in Africa. To represent the goat, my daughters found instructions online on how to fold a towel into the shape of a goat (like the towel animals on cruise ships). If you want to put something in the mail to represent your sponsorship, here are some step-by-step instructions to fold your own goat, origami style: www.origami-instructions.com/origami-goat-face.html.

- *Museum pass.* What a great gift to give to an entire family.

- *Vanilla beans.* Every year I make big batches of vanilla extract by slicing the beans the long way and letting them soak in vodka or rum for at least six weeks. For faraway friends, I will send them bottles of vanilla. But for my Pinterest-type friends (the DIY crowd), I just send some exotic beans through the mail and let them make their own trip to the liquor store. Trust me, your foodie friend will be thrilled.

- *Ebooks*. As an author, I thank you in advance.

- *Audiobooks*. My favorite gift to give—and receive.

- *Magazine subscription*. I know people especially appreciate a subscription renewal for their favorite periodical.

- *Kitchen accessories*. Pot holders, towels, tablecloths, napkins, and cutting boards are flat, easily mailable, and seem to always need replacing.

- *Nationality box*. One year a friend who knew me when I lived in Japan went to a Japanese market and loaded up on popular candies, origami paper, Pocky (a type of cookie dipped in chocolate), cute tissue packs, chopsticks, and stickers. Everything was in pinks and light green, and it was the prettiest package I ever opened.

- *Other ideas*. Here's a random bunch of other ideas to help spark your creativity: superhero cape, bow tie, coffee and tea, nuts, socks, fashion tape, mittens, fabric bags, coasters, cookbooks, decks of cards, and girl stuff (such as hair bands, jewelry, and nail appliqués).

GET SANTA'S WORKSHOP READY

Can you believe you are ten days in? I want you to really, truly enjoy your season. Hopefully, you are:

- somewhat ahead for this year
- totally ahead for next year
- clear about what to get each person on your list
- feeling accomplished

Gather Your Elf Supplies

Originally, this project was going to be "Buy Your Stuff," but I know all of us probably have enough gift wrap, tags, and ribbon to supply Santa's workshop for the next several years. The problem? Most of us find it on December 26.

So, dig through your basement, garage, spare closet, or under the bed and gather together in one place:

- wrapping paper
- ribbon
- tissue paper
- cellophane
- tags, etc.
- Scotch tape
- scissors
- gift bags
- gift boxes

Gather all this into one place so that when you have to go into elf mode, you're not running all over the house. (Or worse—all over Target. In December.)

This would be the time to also purchase anything you are short on (I end up buying tape every single year).

Now, where are you going to keep all those supplies during this season?

MAKE IT A CLUTTER-FREE CHRISTMAS

I would love for you to have an "away space" (in a drawer, a closet, etc.) so all of your Christmas supplies are not on the living room table for the entire month of December.

Do you have a place in your house where you can have easy access to them? A drawer in your dining room or a shelf in your utility closet that is still within reach but isn't in the middle of all the action in your house? That would be the perfect place to stash your stuff. I will be using my coat closet this year because it's close to where I wrap gifts (in the living room).

For all the little things you need to keep together (scissors, tape, tags, etc.), I use a cleaning caddy with a handle that can be easily moved. Having everything together keeps me from putting off wrapping.

Some other wrapping hints:

- *Use it up.* Instead of opening up a brand-new roll of paper, use up all the leftovers of the rolls you have. That way you'll have less to store.

- *Use what you have.* If you have leftover limbs from the tree you cut down, why not tie some of the small branches onto your gifts? Do you have some small ornaments you aren't going to use on your tree? Tie them onto a gift or write on them with a Sharpie to make a festive gift tag.

- *Make photo tags.* Have a photo of Fido you just adore? Make copies and tie them onto your gifts as a fun gift tag everyone will admire.

- *Fabric, ribbons, and buttons.* These are just a few of my favorite things— to decorate packages with. Use up the leftovers from that craft project that just didn't turn out right. Raid the jar of buttons you've been keeping in your laundry room, and glue a couple onto a paper tag to make it festive.

- *Game pieces, candy, old jewelry.* Anything can be turned into a gift tag: Spell out a name with old Scrabble letters, use a deck of cards as gift tags, glue that single earring onto a card, or glue candy kisses onto a bow.

- *Wrap a map.* Use an old map to wrap a gift for the man or travel enthusiast in your life.

The things we do at Christmas

are touched with a

certain extravagance,

as beautiful, in some of its aspects,

as the extravagance of

nature in June.

—Robert Collyer

Elf Supplies

SUPPLIES	HAVE	NEED

Elf Supplies

SUPPLIES	HAVE	NEED

· PROJECT 11 ·

FORGET THE CHRISTMAS LIST— WHAT'S THE CHRISTMAS DINNER LIST?

We've saved a place in this planner for your family favorite recipes! (See pages 84 and 85.) Now is the time to fill up those pages with the traditional treats your family loves.

Each year, our various kids will call or text and *confirm in advance* that we will be preparing their favorite part of the holiday meal. (My kids? Totally have their priorities right.) Here is just a portion of what is on the must-have list:

- cranberry no-bake cheesecake
- pumpkin no-bake cheesecake
- artichoke dip
- bruschetta
- broccoli casserole
- ratatouille
- drunken turkey (turkey brined in white wine and spices)

In years past, I've spent a lot of time and energy going through various cookbooks, computer searches, and junk drawer layers looking for all these recipes—but no more! This year they were all sitting in this little book just where they are supposed to be.

Get Your Recipes Together

The other wonderful thing about having all your recipes together is that when your kids start wanting to take your family recipes to their in-laws' homes, you can copy everything at once.

Who is the most organized woman on the planet?

You are!

Here's what you will need:

> **1.** Gather all the cookbooks, recipe cards, magazine pages, etc. that hold your favorite holiday recipes into one place.
>
> **2.** Put your family's six favorite, must-be-passed-down-for-generations dishes into this book so you (and the rest of your family) will always know where they are.

CLEANING UP YOUR RECIPES

No one gets a prize for collecting the most recipes they will never use. Trim your recipes down to only those you love.

If you have several cookbooks that contain only one or two of your favorite recipes, copy the pages and get rid of the books. Give them to a friend so they can now discover their favorite recipes! By the way, it's perfectly legal to copy recipes out of books you own for your own personal use within your home (because I know some of you were wondering).

I love having all of my holiday recipes on cards in the Magic Christmas Box. I can lay them all out, plan our meals, and make grocery lists, and I don't have to toggle between multiple websites, books, and kitchen drawers. Everything is in one place.

I promise you will thank me for this project when it comes time to get your shopping list together.

ROGER'S NO-BAKE PUMPKIN CHEESECAKE

2 (8 oz.) pkgs. cream cheese

1 cup sugar

1 T. vanilla

1 T. lemon juice

¼ cup pumpkin pie filling

1 premade graham cracker crust

Cinnamon sugar (for garnish)

White chocolate, shaved (for garnish)

Combine the first five ingredients until creamy and fluffy, and then pour the mixture into the graham cracker crust.

Garnish with cinnamon sugar (that makes it look baked) and shaved white chocolate if desired. Refrigerate a few hours before serving.

ROGER'S NO-BAKE CRANBERRY CHEESECAKE

2 (8 oz.) pkgs. cream cheese

1 cup sugar

1 T. vanilla

1 T. lemon juice

1 (14 oz.) can whole berry cranberry sauce, divided

1 premade graham cracker crust

Zest of 1 orange (optional garnish)

White chocolate, shaved (optional garnish)

Combine the cream cheese, sugar, vanilla, lemon juice, and ⅓ cup cranberry sauce together until creamy and fluffy. Pour the mixture into the graham cracker crust.

Garnish with any (or all) of the following: the remaining cranberry sauce (on the outside edge of the pie), orange zest, shaved white chocolate. Refrigerate a few hours before serving.

KATHI'S BRINED TURKEY

1 gallon cold water

1 cup sea salt

1 T. dried rosemary, crushed

1 T. dried sage

1 T. dried thyme

1 bottle dry white wine

3 oranges cut in half

Combine all ingredients in a large garbage bag. Wash and dry the turkey. (Make sure you have removed the innards.) Place the turkey, breast down, into the brine. Make sure the cavity gets filled. Place the bag in a roasting pan and then set in the refrigerator overnight, turning once.

The next day, remove the turkey, carefully draining off the excess brine, and pat dry. Discard the excess brine. Cook the turkey as desired, reserving the drippings for gravy. (Keep in mind that brined turkeys cook 20 to 30 minutes faster, so watch the temperature gauge.)

ARTICHOKE DIP

1 pkg. (8 oz.) cream cheese

1 cup Parmesan cheese, shredded

1 cup mayonnaise (low-fat or fat-free is acceptable)

½ tsp. dill weed

1 clove garlic, crushed

1 (14 oz.) can artichoke hearts, drained and chopped

Preheat the oven to 350°.

Cream the cream cheese, and then add the Parmesan cheese, mayonnaise, dill weed, and garlic. Mix well. Fold in the chopped artichoke hearts and then spoon the mixture into a 9 x 9-inch pan. Bake for 30 minutes.

Serve with crackers, toasted baguettes, or toasted pita points.

BRUSCHETTA

2 T. balsamic vinegar

2 T. fresh herbs, chopped (dill, parsley, basil)

1 baguette, sliced

Goat cheese

Fresh thyme, for garnish

Preheat the broiler to high.

Combine the vinegar and herbs. Place the bread slices on a broiler pan. Char the bread on each side under the hot broiler. (You can also grill the bread if you prefer.) Drizzle the balsamic vinaigrette over the slices of toasted baguette and spread with the goat cheese. Finish with another drizzle of vinaigrette. Garnish with thyme.

Christmas is a necessity.
There has to be at least one day of the year
to remind us that we're here for
something else besides ourselves.

—Eric Severeid

MAKING DO AT CHRISTMAS

One of the aspects I love about traveling so much is the sense of "making do" with what we have while we're on the road.

> I know what it is to be in need, and I know what it is to have plenty. I have learned the secret of being content in any and every situation, whether well fed or hungry, whether living in plenty or in want. I can do all this through him who gives me strength.
>
> **Philippians 4:12-13**

In a cabin in the woods, when we've run out of the meals I planned, I can combine a couple of sausages, a can of beans, and a potato or two to create something magical. Not only do we get to eat something great, but I love the fact that we could make something wonderful out of the bits and pieces we have lying around.

This is the reason I love old quilts so much. Loving hands pieced all the scraps from previous projects together to make something random and beautiful out of what would have been destined for the garbage bin.

What does this have to do with the holidays? I've worked hard to apply the same ideas, notions, and attitude to my Christmas celebration.

Too Much Christmas at the End of the Money

My Christmas will never look like the pages of a magazine or anything on the internet (unless you look at Pinterest fails), and honestly, that used to bother me. I would spend tons of time, energy, and money to try to get the look and feel of that perfect Christmas celebration. As if I could buy my way to a happy holiday.

When my kids became adults, I would stew that they would spend part of their holiday at a friend's house or out of state because of financial reasons (even though I did the same as a young adult).

I used to spend hours I didn't have preparing all the food everyone wanted so everyone would always be happy.

And let's not even talk about the credit cards I did permanent damage to trying to "buy happy" for everyone I had ever met.

But I have come to the realization (after years of banging my head against a Christmas tree) that there is great satisfaction in honoring what you have and not always wishing for more.

Elder Joseph wrote a song called "Simple Gifts" for the Shaker community, who are known for their frugality and simplicity. These are the lyrics to his one-verse song:

'Tis the gift to be simple, 'tis the gift to be free,
'Tis the gift to come down where we ought to be,
And when we find ourselves in the place just right,
'Twill be in the valley of love and delight.
When true simplicity is gained,
To bow and to bend we shan't be ashamed,
To turn, turn will be our delight,
Till by turning, turning we come 'round right.

When I start to go into the Christmas Crazies, I think about this little song and remind myself, the gift isn't more—it's less. To be satisfied with less is a countercultural superpower that will change not only our Christmas celebration but our lives.

Three things have helped me enjoy my Christmas (and my life) immeasurably more:

BEING SATISFIED WITH LESS

This goes for my gift buying, decorating, and even the foods I prepare.

Here are some questions I need to answer each year:

- Do I need to buy new decorations this year, or is this a year to get creative with what I have from last year?

- Do I need to keep everyone on my gift-giving list this year, or are there some who would be relieved not to exchange gifts?

- Do I need to bake a dozen different kinds of cookies, or would our family's three favorites be enough to satisfy everyone?

BEING CREATIVE WITH WHAT I HAVE

One of my favorite decorations each year is taking a few bottom branches of the Christmas tree and tying them together with a plaid ribbon. It's so simple but looks amazing lying on our dark kitchen table.

Taking the decorations you already have and rearranging them in a fresh, new way is so much more satisfying than going out and buying new decorations (or even new materials to make decorations).

BEING COMPLETELY FOCUSED ON WHAT (AND WHOM) I HAVE

One year, living away from home, I was invited to another family's Christmas celebration. The oldest son of the family was living in another country and wasn't able to join them for their celebration.

Or, more accurately, wasn't able to join them for their day of mourning.

You see, the mom was so focused on her son not being there that she couldn't enjoy her daughter who was actually in the room (or her husband, or me, the random guest who was just praying for the "celebration" to end so I could go back to my apartment).

That Christmas was a cautionary tale for me. It's okay to be sad about who's not there, but it's important to focus our love and energy on who is actually in the room.

While I can't have all the people I want at our family celebrations all the time, I'm going to dig in and celebrate the people who are present and let the ones who can't be there know they are missed (without the guilt).

I may not have the decorations of my dreams (or, let's face it, even the house of my dreams), but when the world tells me that in order to be satisfied I always need more, I remember my superpower of being satisfied with less, and I can enjoy what I already have even more.

$\mathcal{M}$aybe Christmas, he thought,

doesn't come from a store.

Maybe Christmas...perhaps...

means a little bit more.

—Dr. Seuss

· PROJECT 13 ·

GET YOUR HGTV ON

Our family members are not collectors of delicate things for multiple reasons.

My mom started a collection for my daughter, Kimber, of figurines called Snowbabies. These statuettes depict small children in snowsuits sledding, skiing, and generally frolicking in the snow. They are made of unglazed porcelain. While I'm not a fan of tiny figurines (I may have been traumatized by the "no-touch" policy of the Hummels of my youth), these are actually pretty cute.

Every year, not only would Kimber look forward to receiving a new one, but her collection of Snowbabies was the first thing she went to unpack as we started to decorate for Christmas.

Lacking a mantel in our home, I hung all of our stockings on a shelf in the playroom/office/ dining room of our tiny house. After hanging the stockings, I covered the shelf in snow-like fluff and nestled the six Snowbabies among the snow to create our own little winter wonderland.

Until later that day when I heard the *crash*.

My son, Justen, hoping Santa had come a little early to fill the stockings with gummy bears, decided to tug his stocking down to see what was inside. Along with the stocking, Justen pulled down the entire shelf, and all those Snowbabies hurtled to the floor.

And this is just one of the many examples of why we don't have nice things...

To this day, we still display those Snowbabies, but now they are more customized for our family. Let's just say that figurine restoration is not one of my giftings. Those Snowbabies have some bumps and bruises, but they are survivors. That makes us love them a little bit more.

Décor Day

Here is what you will need:

- Your Christmas décor boxes from last year

- A Christmas tree removal bag (You can purchase these at any hardware store or general store, like Target. These bags keep you from getting pine needles all over your floor when you take the tree down and drag it to the curb. The trick— remembering to put it around the base of the tree when you first put the tree up!) I buy these several at a time, and it's the last thing I pack up before packing away the boxes, so it will be the first thing I see when unpacking the boxes next year.

- Ornament hooks

Here are some of the things you may want to consider working on:

- Get and decorate your tree.

- Put away some of your everyday stuff so you'll have room for your Christmas décor.

- Swap out your regular dishes for your Christmas dishes.

- Decorate outside.

MAKE IT A CLUTTER-FREE CHRISTMAS

Let It Go

One of the big helps for Christmas décor is to get rid of anything you are no longer decorating with—those pink snowmen you bought during your *Miami* Christmas phase, or that stack of Christmas cards from people you no longer connect with. The less you have to sort through, the easier the decorating process will be.

Treasure or Trash

If you have broken ornaments, today would be a great day to get out the superglue and repair them. If they aren't worthy of the time it will take to fix 'em, pitch 'em.

Repurpose for Christmas

You don't need to redecorate your entire house for the holidays. I have some awesome wood-and-glass bird cages that are in my living room all year long. Instead of taking them down for Christmas, I fill them up with some inexpensive Christmas bulbs. I love them so much that I kept them up through February this year.

Every year I take a plain door in our house (this year it's the door to our furnace) and wrap it like a big present. Then as Christmas cards come into the house, I tape them directly to the door. I save the envelopes in a Ziploc bag in my Magic Christmas Box to check for new addresses.

As I'm unpacking holiday decorations, I do two things:

1. I pull out anything I'm not planning to decorate with and set it aside to give away. I would much rather my Christmas décor end up at a charity shop in November or December than in January when I'm packing it all away. Wouldn't it be great if some family was able to decorate their tree this year because you are so organized and on top of it?

2. As I pull out the décor, I use those empty containers that have held all my decorations to hold some of the home décor I have out the other ten months of the year.

Get the rest of your décor in the holiday mood. I have three fat ceramic chickens that Roger bought me on our first anniversary. I love those chickens too much to put them away at Christmas, so I give each of them a red bow for the holidays, and they fit right in.

✴ WHEN IT NEEDS TO BE A SIMPLE CHRISTMAS ✴

You could have a million reasons why you are so time crunched this Christmas—family obligation, a huge project at work. Here's one question I would ask you to consider: Do you feel a time crunch every Christmas? If so, I strongly recommend that you not only make some accommodations this year, but take a hard look at your expectations for the holiday season.

Sometimes we are afraid of making changes because we're sure that everyone is going to be disappointed by what we're not doing. The reality probably is that we're doing a lot of things that are important only to us, and possibly only for tradition's sake.

Here is what I've learned about time and Christmas:

1. *You need to ask your family what is important.* Immediately stop doing anything your family doesn't find important to their own holiday celebration.

2. *You are the one putting the most pressure on you.* Most of us have some picture of what Christmas should look like, but I'm guessing that much of what that picture contains could be done away with when times are hard. Do you need a full-blown Christmas tree, or would a tiny one that sits on your mantel do? Do you need to have the turkey with all the trimmings, or would a Christmas dinner of Chinese takeout be okay for a year when you aren't up to cooking?

3. *Everyone gets a pass.* Give yourself a pass—and the rest of the people in your life a pass as well. Have the conversation. Because both my husband and I had surgeries within a month of Christmas one year, I told my extended family that we were happy to host, but I would not be buying or cooking the entire meal. My mom wasn't in a position to host, but she was happy to shop and cook for us at my house with the help of all the kids. Everyone contributed, and no one was stretched.

4. *The saying, "It just won't be Christmas without…" must be banned from your vocabulary.* The only thing you need in order to celebrate Christmas is a relationship with your Savior. I'm not trying to get all Phariseeish here, but we must remember that everything else is the fudge on the ice cream that is our true reason for celebrating. Don't make yourself crazy with ideas like "It just won't be Christmas if I don't put all the ornaments on the tree," or "It just won't be Christmas if we don't see *The Nutcracker* this year." Yes, it will still be Christmas. It will just be a Christmas where you aren't stretching yourself too thin.

5. *Changing traditions gives you freedom.* So you put up a tree with lights only, no ornaments (like we are doing this year). Think how much fun it's going to be to see those ornaments next year! Tradition can be a merciless slave driver.

Give yourself and the people you love the gift of time this year by dropping the expectations that no longer serve you. Enjoy more of the Christmas pastimes that make you happy.

THE SENSES OF THE SEASON

BY KARIANNE WOOD

 If Christmas had a fan club, I would be president.

Or vice president.

Or hospitality chairperson.

I can't help it. Christmas is the season for giving and decking the halls and carols and making and baking and wishing and hoping and celebrating the birth of a tiny child that took place more than 2,000 years ago on a starry night in a lowly manger. A night when the heavens rang and the angels sang and a weary world rejoiced together in perfect harmony because a king had finally arrived.

The night a savior was born.

I want my home to be a reflection of our Savior's love for us. I want to create a safe haven from the busy of the season. I want friends and family alike to be surrounded by the love and joy and peace the Christmas season brings. Simply put, I want to deck the halls with my Christmas heart. And so? I decorate for each of the five senses.

Brilliant. Right?

One of my official duties as a member of the Christmas fan club is to spread joy and decorating cheer. Here is a list of the five senses and how to decorate for each one.

 Sight. This is where most Christmas decorating begins and ends—and it all starts with the tree. Tree decorating doesn't have to be expensive. Handmade ornaments are the best. Paint wood slices with family member's names and tie them on the tree with a ribbon. Swirl paint inside of clear glass globes for a one-of-a-kind ornament. Trace the words to a favorite carol onto yards of burlap ribbon and deck the tree for Christmas morning.

2 *Sound.* Nothing says Christmas like a familiar carol. Put together a playlist of your favorite Christmas carols and then set it on repeat. Old favorites mixed with new songs create instant Christmas cheer.

3 *Taste.* I wish I could tell you I was a brilliant Christmas baker whose Christmas cookies were legendary. Truth? Umm…not so much. My Christmas cookies come from the bakery. For those of us who are baking challenged, here's an idea to have your cookies and eat them too: Host a cookie exchange. Each guest brings six or eight dozen of one kind of cookie, and then everyone swaps.

4 *Touch.* Introduce texture this Christmas. Toss a chunky knitted throw over the back of a chair. Place a marble cutting board layered with cheese and crackers on the kitchen counter. Fill chairs with soft, fuzzy pillows, and hang knitted stockings on the mantel to add depth and texture to your Christmas décor.

5 *Smell.* Ahh. The most Christmassy of all the senses. The smell of fresh pine added to a wreath on the door. The scent of apple cider–filled mugs in the kitchen. The scent of cinnamon on freshly baked Christmas cookies.

Wrapping yourself and your home with the sights, sounds, tastes, textures, and smells of the season creates a Christmas treat for the senses.

Are you ready to decorate?

Want to join the Christmas fan club too?

Oh, good.

We're accepting applications.

· PROJECT 14 ·

THE CHEW HAS NOTHING ON YOU

My kids still tell the story—15 years later—of the day we didn't eat Christmas dinner. It's part of our family history. Do I regret my mistake? No. (I'd do almost anything for a good story.) But I've learned from that mistake, and we will never, ever have 12 appetizers again.

I knew I should have made a list. My work schedule had been crazy, and we had loads of family coming over for Christmas Eve. I knew what I wanted to cook for our dinner—a big ham with all the sides: potatoes, both scalloped and mashed, green bean casserole, salad, stuffing, rolls (can you tell we love our carbs?), cranberry sauce, and asparagus. Yes, it was going to be an amazing meal.

> ***
> I knew I should have made a list.

I was handling the ham and all the sides. So when my mom asked what she could bring, I told her, "Could you bring some appetizers?" She said, "No problem." A few weeks later, as we got closer to our celebration, my brother asked what he could bring. Knowing I had the main meal covered, I said, "How about a few hors d'oeuvres?"

And then my in-laws asked what they could bring. Knowing that dinner would take a while, I asked them to bring a few snacks to help tide us over until the meal would be ready. And in case anyone was late, I prepared a few cheese-and-cracker plates and made some artichoke dip.

The day of the meal, after we all gathered together and spent the next several hours grazing through all the prefood, no one ate a bite of dinner. Not. One. Bite.

Now, there may be a day in the future where we decide to have an all-appetizer Christmas meal. (In fact, that sounds like an amazing idea. The wheels in my head are turning…) But a little planning and a list on the fridge would have saved us from a lot of waste—and me from being the central character in "The Christmas Dinner That Never Got Eaten."

A little planning up front can save you from such disasters.

Prep Your Kitchen

Today's project is to spend a little more time in the kitchen. Here are some things you may want to get ahead on:

- Create your "every night" meal plan for the rest of the holiday season. Keep it simple but healthy. Why not cook up a big pot of soup you can eat over several meals? Plan out what you'll eat on the nonholidays so you can focus your creativity on the big, fun meals.

- Plan out your Christmas dinner and your shopping list. Do this early so you have a plan and can work your plan (and can flex as more people are coming to dinner and offer to bring dishes).

- Shop for nonperishables. Buy these as soon as you know what you need. I put all of them in a storage container in our garage so I don't accidentally use something I need to make pumpkin pie (and feel the wrath of my whole family as we celebrate a pie-less holiday).

- Make a list of what you need to buy at the last minute so it's fresh.

- Set up a grocery delivery to get all those last-minute items (fresh fruits and veggies, etc.) delivered to your door (and avoid the grocery store—score!).

- Pull out your serving platters, roasting pans, cake stands, or anything else you'll need.

- Create your baking list.

Not only are we a blended family, but we are starting to add some new family members. Shaun and Amanda have been married for a few years now, and my daughter, Kimber, has a serious boyfriend. So not only do our kids have another parent to split the holiday with, but we are also dealing with significant others' families and making it work.

Our new plan these past few years has been to have one

big, traditional meal each year, and then we do something fun and different for the other holidays.

For instance, one year we had everyone at our house for Thanksgiving (including some friends and our new neighbors from China), and we made the turkey, ham, potatoes, stuffing, rolls, salad, and pies. Lots of pies.

But for our Christmas celebration, we went much simpler: pizza fondue. In years past? We've barbecued, made a big pot of chili and homemade bread, ravioli, and tamales. Sometimes the best thing you can do is pick a theme and go with it. Maybe it's a crab boil or lasagna. But keeping it simple and different from your other holidays is the idea.

This past Christmas may have been the best of them all. We had a raclette party. Raclette is a cheese from Switzerland, and it is served melted. We actually bought an electric tabletop grill specifically for melting the cheese. We also used the grill to heat up small potatoes, dried meat, cocktail onions, and gherkin pickles. It sounds strange, but trust me, it was amazing. Our whole family agreed that it was their favorite Christmas meal. (And bonus for the host: Everything is done in advance and then it's completely DIY.)

> *** * ***
>
> I ask each family member this one simple question: What is the one dish that you *must* have for Christmas?

But there are times when we just want to go classic. So when it's time to do the traditional dinner, I ask each family member this one simple question: What is the one dish that you *must* have for Christmas?

That way, we can make sure that everyone has their favorites.

I keep all our traditional family favorite recipes in this book, and if I see anything interesting I'd like to try, I'll print it and throw it in the Magic Christmas Box. That way, when I sit down to plan, I have everything in one place and don't have to waste time or paper reprinting recipes.

Here are some of the things I like to do in advance if I will be hosting our huge Christmas dinner (or a lot of little celebrations along the way):

- I make a calendar of all the events we'll be hosting, along with any event that we'll be attending that we are bringing food to. This helps me wrap my head around all the extras we'll be doing this season, and it helps me estimate the amount we'll need to put aside budget-wise for the next several weeks.

- If I'm going to be attending a lot of parties, I try to sign up to bring the same dish to each one. It's far easier to bring our famous artichoke dip to four different parties than to come up with four different dishes (and so far, no one has ever turned down our artichoke dip).

- After you make a list of everything you will need throughout the season, go through your cupboards and pantry to see what you already have instead of buying everything on your list. You may have all the canned pumpkin you need left over from your fall baking kick.

  Check your inventory re:

  * Ziploc bags
  * aluminum foil
  * plastic wrap
  * to-go containers (for giving friends and family leftovers and not being bitter and resentful when they hold your Snapware hostage for the next three years)
  * paper towels

- And my best advice? When someone offers to bring a dish, let them. But just keep track of what you've asked people to bring. Unless you really like appetizers. Then, hey! Live dangerously.

Christmas Eve Meals

APPETIZERS

....
....
....
....
....

MAIN DISH

....
....
....
....
....

SIDES AND SALADS

....
....
....
....
....

DRINKS

....
....
....
....
....

BREAD AND ROLLS

....
....
....
....
....

DESSERTS

....
....
....
....
....

Christmas Day Meals

APPETIZERS

....

....

....

....

....

MAIN DISH

....

....

....

....

....

SIDES AND SALADS

....

....

....

....

....

DRINKS

....

....

....

....

....

BREAD AND ROLLS

....

....

....

....

....

DESSERTS

....

....

....

....

....

· PROJECT 15 ·

ON THE TWELFTH DAY OF CHRISTMAS, MY TRUE LOVE BROUGHT TO ME... 12 BOTTLES OF HAND SANITIZER

I come from a family who raced downstairs at the crack of dawn to flip our stockings upside down and riffle through our big pile of loot. It was just the way it was done. So, naturally, on our first Christmas together as man and wife with Roger, I ran—I mean, walked with purpose and elegance—down the stairs and dumped my stocking to find...nothing.

Turns out, Roger's ex-wife had been the keeper of the stockings at his house.

It really didn't bother me (I promise), but I think Roger felt bad. So the next year, he informed me that he had bought something for my stocking. And I raced—I mean, walked like an adult—down the stairs to dump my stocking to find...12 bottles of hand sanitizer.

Twelve bottles.

It was the cute Bath and Body Works hand sanitizer.

But it was still hand sanitizer.

His heart was in the right place.

Again, I wasn't offended (after all, hand sanitizer has its place). But I made a promise to myself: Every year, I was going to buy myself something special for my own stocking—nothing big or extravagant, but maybe a lotion I've been wanting or a pair of earrings. A little Christmas treat for myself.

And, I have to admit, I'm pretty good at playing Santa.

Get Those Stockings Ready

Today's project is to get ready for stockings at your house. (Don't worry, you don't have to do all the shopping today, but you do have to get ready for it.) Here's what I want you to do:

Come Up with a Plan

It's really easy to go overboard (or underboard) with stockings. So my first suggestion is to come up with a plan on what you want to buy and how much you want to spend. For example, maybe your plan is to spend $25 on each stocking and get eight items for each person. Or maybe this is the year where you have more creativity than cash. Start thinking through all the ideas you want to put into play to make your stockings rock without a lot of dough.

Come Up with a System

In my gift closet, I keep a resealable bag for each person with their name on it. As I gather up little treats for each person, I wrap them and keep them in the appropriate bag. When it comes time to fill the individual stockings, all I do is dump the contents of each bag into the appropriate stocking.

Shop Slowly but Surely

Going shopping for stocking stuffers all at once can be daunting. I make it a point to pick up little things I see throughout the year and slip them into those handy resealable bags. That said, if you haven't already started, make it your goal to pick up one or two things for stockings each time you go shopping from now until Christmas, and you will slowly whittle away at your list.

For years I bought little toys and treats just so the stockings would be full. But there's a reason those things at the entrance to Target are only a dollar—that's about how much you will use the item (a dollar's worth) before it becomes a piece of clutter in your room, or more likely, your kid's room. When thinking about stocking stuffers, only buy things you don't mind cleaning up later. In other words, buy things that are small and will be loved and used. Keep them practical, useful, and fun.

> ✳✳✳
> Make it your goal to pick up one or two things for stockings each time you go shopping, and you will slowly whittle away at your list.

On this project, instead of giving you quick tips, I'm going to list 40 fabulous, fun, and festive stocking stuffer ideas. Enjoy.

1. chocolate gold coins
2. mini flashlights (these are a huge hit at our house)
3. USB cords
4. toothbrushes (we include these every year)
5. fun flavors of K-Cup coffee pods
6. hair things (rubber bands or barrettes)
7. playing cards
8. thank-you notes (these are supposed to inspire the kids to actually write the notes… it happens about 50 percent of the time…under threat of having all their other gifts taken away)
9. nail polish
10. anything Burt's Bees
11. Starbucks gift cards
12. little jars of syrup, jam, or jelly
13. small tools (what guy doesn't want a cute little screwdriver to carry around in his car?)

14. lip balm (I love EOS Smooth Sphere lip balms)
15. nice pens (I love the Uniball Air pen)

16. gum or mints
17. hand sanitizer (perhaps not 12 bottles, though)
18. fun spices or spice mixes
19. portable charger
20. AA or AAA batteries (I would be thrilled to get a pack of these in my stocking)
21. fun socks (my son gets a pair of Star Wars socks every year…he REALLY looks forward to those socks)

22. earbuds

23. essential oils

24. Post-it Notes

25. packages of hot chocolate mix

26. an Itty Bitty Book Light

27. razor

28. tweezers

29. facial mask

30. cosmetic brush set

31. Moleskine mini notebook

32. Amazon gift cards for books

33. movie tickets

34. travel containers of shampoo, body wash, or conditioner

35. a journal

36. a favorite candy from the person's childhood

37. trading cards (baseball or football or Pokémon)

38. a specialty chocolate bar (bonus points if you find a flavor like maple bacon or chili lime)

39. an orange (it smells wonderful and fits nicely in the toe of a stocking)

40. travel-sized games (mini magnetic board games work great)

One reader suggested a themed stocking (love that!). Here are some ideas for you to choose from:

- gardening
- office supplies
- reading
- camping
- travel

WRAPPED OR UNWRAPPED?

This is a personal preference, but I'm a renegade and do a combination of wrapped and unwrapped. I love variety.

If you wrap, wrap as you go, and then you won't be up the night before Christmas chained to your elf work desk.

REFRESH YOURSELF

Whew. You've been working hard, haven't you?

The Christmas season is always a frantic array of hustle and bustle. It's enough to sometimes make you want to scream. Literally.

I remember a day last year when I had a teensy bit too much on my to-do list. And by that, I mean I had attempted to not only go shopping for gifts for 14 people, but I also thought it might be a good idea to go grocery shopping for nonperishables, buy my wrapping paper, go to the post office, and stop by the church office to deliver muffins. All on the same day. Oh, and I also had to work.

> ✳✳✳
> We all need a break
> this time of year.

I realized at about 4:00 that I'd attempted too much when I snapped at Roger for no apparent reason. And Roger—bless his heart—just sat me down and said we needed a *How I Met Your Mother* marathon night. So we snuggled on the couch, ate take-out, and watched TV for about 13 billion hours. And the next morning, guess what happened? Good Kathi came back.

And I was able to make it through my now way-more-realistic to-do list without a single meltdown.

We all need a break this time of year. So today, before you get to that point of no return, your project is to do something really fun just for yourself.

Get Some You Time

I know it's hard to find time for you, especially during the holidays. I also know that you may be tempted to skip this project because women are notoriously unselfish and are often willing to sacrifice whatever time or money that could be for themselves for their family. But I'm not letting you out of this. You need this. And you will be a better mom, wife, friend, and elf this holiday season if you take some time for yourself.

So your job today is to find one way to refresh yourself. I've listed some ideas below to get you started, but use your imagination and do something that you know will help you wake up tomorrow feeling ready to face the day. And to face Project 17.

REFRESH YOURSELF IDEAS

- Take a bubble bath.
- Spend an hour reading a great novel by the fire.
- Go on a long walk in the park (even better if you can invite a friend to go with you).
- Grab lunch or coffee with a friend.
- Grab lunch or coffee by yourself and revel in the silence.
- Pick up a cupcake or a brownie and enjoy every single bite.
- Get a makeover at the mall.
- Call a friend and talk for as long as you can about whatever you want.
- Go on a date night with your man.
- Watch a Christmas movie.
- Make a Christmas playlist and blast it through your speakers all day long.
- Sit in front of the Christmas tree and just think and pray.

And if you want to do something for Christmas, make sure it's something you really want to do. If you love making beautiful things, arts and crafts it up! If you love to bake, get elbow deep in some cookie dough—just make sure it's something that you really, really want to do.

Because you deserve it.

· PROJECT 17 ·

WHEN SANTA WON'T DELIVER

I'm not one to cry in public, but the post office at Christmastime is enough to make a grown woman weep. And then binge on candy canes. (I know this from experience.)

A few years ago, before I discovered the magic of USPS.com (more on that later), I made the entirely unwise choice to brave the post office on December 16 while I was a) hungry and b) tired.

It didn't look bad when I walked in. Just 20-odd people in line, a few boxes lining the edges of the building. But as I stood there watching the line creep to the front with record-breaking slowness, I realized I had been mistaken. Because not only did each person in front of me have at least 243 packages to ship, but each of them was also cranky, tired, and as ready to get out of there as I was.

Oh, and they were happy to tell the postal workers about their angst when they finally got to the front of the line, adding a good five minutes to each person's already excruciatingly long turn.

There is a better way, ladies. And today I'm going to tell you about it so you can get all of those packages shipped to your loved ones in plenty of time for them to *ooh* and *aah* at them under the tree.

And just think of how great you'll feel to get through shipping day without eating a single candy cane. (Well, have one. Let's not go crazy here…)

> ***
> A few years ago, I made the entirely unwise choice to brave the post office on December 16 while I was a) hungry and b) tired.

Ho! Ho! Ho! To the Post Office You Go!

Get all of your packages shipped out today, and if you forgot someone, don't worry. Tomorrow is online shopping day, so you can finish up then.

MAKE IT EASY ON YOURSELF

I have two tips I think will make today's project one of your easiest ones:

> 1. Learn how to ship using USPS.com (they have a whole shipping guide if you've never done it before).
>
> 2. Use Priority Mail boxes.

Why do I love those Priority Mail boxes so?

Guys, I could write an ode to Priority Mail boxes. I use them every day in my business, but they really become heroes around the holidays. Why?

You can schedule Priority Mail to be picked up at your house the next day.

Right? Isn't that amazing?

You go to the website at USPS.com, put in some info, pay for the labels, put them on your boxes, and leave them on your front porch for your postal carrier to pick up the next day.

Glorious.

Or, if you have a problem with porch pirates (guys who come by your house and help themselves to your packages…grrr…), those same prepaid, preprinted boxes can just be dropped off at the post office, and you don't need to wait in line. You can just go up to the front counter and drop them off…like a boss.

(My personal advice: Have someone drive you to the post office while you jump out of the car with the packages, drop them off at the counter, and jump back into the car. I mean, you don't even have to deal with parking. It's a Christmas miracle…)

I like to use the Priority Mail boxes that you don't have to weigh—those prepaid boxes you can just keep stuffing until you can barely close them, and the rate stays the same.

Oh, happy days.

- Wrap a bunch of smaller gifts and then place them in a Priority Mail box to send to one family.

- You can't send anything liquid or fragile, so make sure your gifts meet postal service requirements before you wrap them.

May the fire of this log warm the cold;

may the hungry be fed;

may the weary find rest,

and may all enjoy Heaven's peace.

Traditional prayer said when
Yule log is lighted

SHOPPING IN YOGA PANTS

I intended to be one of the last holdouts.

I was going to go to the actual stores and handpick my gifts, and I was going to wrap them and box them and label them and then stand in the hours-long line at the post office to ship them for my loved ones.

This was "walking both ways uphill to school in the snow" material, you guys. But I was going to stick with it. And do it well. Because my friends and family needed personally taped and shipped boxes from me, for the love of all that is holy.

But then this little thing called Amazon Prime was released. And, oh my word, I could click a little button, and in two days, the box magically arrived at my loved one's house with a little gift note. For free. And all I had to do was kick back in my desk chair, wearing jammies and drinking a skinny vanilla latte, and find something awesome to send.

I'll just come out and say it. This has changed me. Online shopping has made me a better gift giver. A better shopper. And honestly, a better human being because I'm way less cranky at the end of the day when I don't have to stand in line at the mall or the post office.

For today's project, I'm going to have you finish up your shopping online. Sure, you can still pick up that extra-special something for your husband at that cute little chocolate shop down the road, but for distant family members and such, today is your day to get your shopping done.

Get Online

Of course, not everyone has Amazon Prime, and not every perfect gift is available through Amazon's website, so before you do your online shopping, I want to make sure you know the best places to shop online. I asked my readers, and they submitted dozens of fantastic "fishing holes" so we can all be faster, cheaper, better this year.

Here are a few favorite ideas, both mine and from them.

- Zulily is a flash sale site that has adorable things for kids, women, and the home all on sale for at least 30 percent off. There is a catch: Zulily is notoriously slow at shipping, but they do have a little gift icon on items they guarantee by Christmas, so I would stick to those.

- Zappos offers free shipping and free returns of clothes, shoes, and household goods.

- Amazon printable gift cards. In case you forgot to get your father-in-law a gift (Who, me? Never.), you can pop on there and send him a gift card that will arrive in his inbox on Christmas morning, as if you'd planned it that way all along. You can even e-mail him a list of your favorite book suggestions to go with the gift card.

- If you're buying for a group of people, think of a food treat they could all share. Vermont Brownie Company makes the best brownies I have ever tasted, and they ship everywhere.

- Have a foodie in your life? Try a locally produced food item to be delivered. Last year for Christmas, I sent many of my friends garlic products or Cowgirl Creamery cheeses, both local to me here in Silicon Valley. Local and the best cheese I've ever tasted.

- Write a list of whom you are shopping for and how much you want to spend for each person before you sit down to online shop. (You could use the Budgeting Sheets on pages 48 and 49.) It's easy to get carried away when you're online, so it's important to have a game plan.

- Use RetailMeNot to search out a coupon code before you check out at each place.

- If a site has a deal like "spend $50, get free shipping," try to buy two presents there. Most places will ship your purchases to different locations.

Notes for Best Places to Shop Online

MY FAVORITE PLACES

....

....

....

....

....

....

....

....

....

....

....

....

....

....

Notes for Best Places to Shop Online

PLACES MY FAMILY AND FRIENDS RECOMMEND

....

....

....

....

....

....

....

....

....

....

....

....

....

....

· PROJECT 19 ·

TAKE OFF YOUR APRON AND GRAB YOUR PENCIL

I've been known to nail Christmas dinner.

What can I say? I love to cook, and I love to plan. Generally, I plan the meal long in advance, get all the recipes printed and ingredients gathered, and make a pretty amazing meal for my family on the big day.

But the weeks leading up to Christmas? Well, let's just say that Roger has been known to affectionately call them "the cereal days." I cook dinner nearly every night all year long, but prior to Christmas I become sidetracked planning for the big day and forget about all the days leading up to it.

And so we eat…well, cereal. And yogurt. And crackers and cheese.

But a few years ago, I made a promise to myself that I would not be that person anymore. You know, the one who pulls out all the stops for company but grumbles at my husband when he asks if there is any Raisin Bran while I'm trying to make the broccoli casserole for all our guests. (Poor guy, he's just trying to stave off starvation…) And so now I started planning our pre-Christmas meals way ahead. Like before Thanksgiving ahead. It seemed a bit crazy at the time, but here's what I ended up doing as a result of my early planning:

- I chopped up leftover Thanksgiving turkey and separated it into one- and two-cup bags. I froze these and used them to add to turkey noodle soup, casseroles, enchiladas, and more.

- Every time I cooked in early-to-mid December, I made sure to cook a LeftOvers On Purpose (LOOP) meal. That way I was able to freeze some extra meals for those busy days.

- In the days right before Christmas, I planned simple, wholesome meals that would feed us well without costing a ton.

***
Create your meal plan for from now until Christmas. Yes, for that long.

You know what? It was magical.

I had dinner—a real dinner—on the table every night, and I still had time to obsess over the chicken crepes recipe my mom makes for the big day. And because this was so helpful to me, your project for today is to do some meal planning—not just for your Christmas dinner, but also for the days that come before. (Trust me, the Tuesday before Thanksgiving, when you're not eating Frosted Flakes with a side of canned string beans, you'll thank me…)

Spend Some Time in the Kitchen

Today's project is to spend a little more time in the kitchen—but there's a catch. I don't want you to bake any cookies, prep any casseroles, or even make a freezer meal. What I want you to do is create your meal plan for from now until Christmas. Yes, for that long. Because the next couple of weeks will be crazy busy, but your family still has to eat. (Those monsters…)

Won't it be nice to have a bunch of easy, healthy meals planned ahead? So today, take off your apron, grab a piece of paper (or a stack of Post-it Notes), and take the time to:

- Create your meal plan for the rest of the month. Use the calendar page for December on page 105. Yes, I know it's a lot, but figure out what you're going to have for dinner every night from now until Christmas.

- Make your baking list so you know what you need to bake and when you're going to do it.

- Plan out your Christmas dinner.

- Write a shopping list for all the meals, your baking, and Christmas dinner. Divide the list into two parts—the nonperishables and the perishables.

- Shop for your nonperishables and the next few days' meals. If you don't have time today, put a date on the calendar for when you will do this.

- Make a list of the things you'll need to buy at the last minute so they are fresh.

MAKE IT EASY ON YOUR CHRISTMAS SELF

Plan on making at least two LOOP meals a week. Cook twice, eat four times.

Use up what you have. We have a motto around our house that we say whenever we're planning dinner, grabbing a snack, or looking for something to put on our oatmeal: "Fresh First!" This means our goal is to use up our fresh ingredients so we're not throwing away pounds of carrots or letting heads of lettuce rot in the fridge. Then we make it a goal to use up any food in our freezer and pantry by the end of the year. Besides, eating from your existing stock is much cheaper and will help with the extra expenses during the holidays. It's a total win-win.

Even if your meal plan is grilled cheese or PB and J, write it down. It will feel good to have a plan.

If your freezer is already running low, pick up some good-quality frozen meals (or make your own) so you always have something to pull out of the freezer.

When in doubt, make soup. I can almost always make a decent soup out of whatever leftovers I have at home.

Check out my book *The "What's for Dinner?" Solution* for good recipes for LOOP meals and freezer meals.

Go easy on yourself for Christmas dinner. Yes, that recipe that has three weeks' worth of steps and 43 ingredients looks delicious, but I'm guessing the much simpler recipe with half the steps and a quarter of the ingredients will make your tummy full and your heart happy.

Christmas QUICK TIPS

May you never be too grown up

to search the skies on Christmas Eve.

— Author Unknown

Planning and Shopping Lists

PERISHABLES

....

....

....

....

....

....

....

....

....

....

NONPERISHABLES

....

....

....

....

....

....

....

....

....

....

LAST MINUTE ITEMS

....

....

....

....

....

....

....

....

DECEMBER MEALS

SUNDAY	MONDAY	TUESDAY	WEDNESDAY	THURSDAY	FRIDAY	SATURDAY
☐	☐	☐	☐	☐	☐	☐
☐	☐	☐	☐	☐	☐	☐
☐	☐	☐	☐	☐	☐	☐
☐	☐	☐	☐	☐	☐	☐
☐	☐	☐	☐	☐	☐	☐

· PROJECT 20 ·

TABLECLOTHS, NAPKINS, AND FOOF, OH MY

I'm still notorious for what I affectionately call the "Thomas the Tank Engine Christmas."

It was the pre-Pinterest era, which meant that we had to get all our holiday ideas from magazines and books. But I had done it. After scouring *Good Housekeeping* and *Sunset*, I had come up with a plan for a beautiful holiday table. I bought a centerpiece with red poinsettias and silver ribbons. I had little pinecones scattered on the perfectly pressed tablecloth. And I had Thomas the Tank Engine napkins.

Yes, I had forgotten to buy napkins. And not only that, but I had also inconveniently run out of plain white paper towels and dinner napkins. My lovely red cloth napkins were lost somewhere in the attic, and after 45 minutes of looking on Christmas Eve, I gave up. So all I had were Thomas the Tank Engine napkins left over from Justen's birthday party.

And it was fine—really—but oh, what I would have done to have pretty little red napkins on my beautiful table.

Which is why today's project is for you to get your table settings for your holiday dinner planned out so everything is ready for the big event.

> ✳✳✳
>
> All you have to do is find all the stuff you need for your table setting right now so you have one less thing to fuss with on Christmas Day.

Get Your Table Stuff All Ready

Today, I'm going to help you avoid the mad scramble on December 25 to find all the napkins, rings, tablecloths, and foof to make your dinner table look beautiful.

This project doesn't need a ton of explanation. All you really have to do is find all the stuff you need for your table setting right now so you have one less thing to fuss with on Christmas Day.

So, set down this book and go and find:

- tablecloths (If they need ironing, you can be an overachiever and iron them.)
- napkins

- table runners
- napkin rings
- Christmas plates
- silverware

Even if you are doing paper or plastic this year, write a list of what you will need so you can purchase those items way in advance and don't have to make a last-minute trip to the store.

KEEP IT SIMPLE

Instead of hanging on to Christmas napkins for another eleven months, we use up any open packages of paper napkins, plates, or cups in January. Less clutter to deal with and store.

For our main dinner plates, I have 24 clear glass plates I bought 13 years ago at IKEA for a buck each. They go with everything, look pretty on a table, and save on hassle. I use them for every holiday and anytime we have more than eight people over for a meal. I have never regretted that purchase.

- If you see napkins, paper plates, or cups on sale, pick up extras.

- Use the same table settings each year. I know something new and awesome is always on Pinterest, and I know it's fun to change things up, but I suggest you get nice, basic stuff (a white tablecloth and red plates, for example) and then use your creativity with centerpieces and extras.

- Store all your table settings in one bin so they're easy to find and get out.

- Keep your table simple. The fun of the meal is togetherness, not fanciness (oh…and the food).

- Add one new table decoration to your things each year. Last year, my mom made me a quilted table runner that looks great with my plates. This year, I plan to buy new napkin rings. That way, you can have something fresh and new on your table without spending a fortune.

And after him came next the chill December:

Yet he, through merry feasting which he made

And great bonfires, did not the cold remember;

His Saviour's birth his mind so much did glad.

— Spenser

YOUR PERSONALIZED SPECIAL PROJECT

For years I have wanted to make my kids a tape of Christmas music. Back before iTunes playlists or even CD burners, we had to use one of those fancy dual cassette recorders (please say I'm not the only one who remembers these) to make new tapes.

Anyway, back when my kids were little, we used to blast Christmas music in my car during the holiday season. We all grew very attached to certain songs, such as those on Bing Crosby's Christmas album (swoon), and I've often thought about how fun it would be to make my kids a tape of our favorite Christmas songs from their childhoods.

> ***
>
> Think of your own special task that you have wanted to do for years but have never had time for. Today is your day to do that thing.

But I've never had the time, much less the technical wherewithal, to get it done. (Those dual cassette recordings were easy compared to iTunes.) But this year, because everything else is done early (thank you, Christmas projects), I decided to make this happen.

I had to recruit Roger's help, but I was able to put together a really cool playlist of favorite Christmas songs for each of my kids. Both of them were really excited to get it, and it felt so special to do something that was so...us.

For your last project, I want you to think of your own special task that you have wanted to do for years but have never had time for. Maybe it's a tradition you want to start for your family, a surprise gift you want to pull off for one of your kids, or even a special holiday date night for your husband.

Today is your day to do that thing.